T0012421

IN RECITAL™
Throughout the Year
(with Performance Strategies)

Volume One

ABOUT THE SERIES • A NOTE TO THE TEACHER

In Recital™ — *Throughout the Year* is a series that focuses on fabulous repertoire, intended to motivate your students. We know that to motivate, the teacher must challenge the student with attainable goals. This series makes that possible. The fine composers and arrangers of this series have created musically engaging pieces, which have been carefully leveled and address the technical strengths and weaknesses of students. The wide range of styles in each book of the series complements other FJH publications and will help you to plan students' recital repertoire for the entire year. You will find original solos and duets that focus on different musical and technical issues, giving you the selection needed to accommodate your students' needs. There are arrangements of famous classical themes, as well as repertoire written for Halloween, Christmas, and Fourth of July recitals. In this way, your student will have recital pieces throughout the entire year! Additionally, the series provides a progressive discussion on the art of performance. The earlier levels offer tips on recital preparation, while the later levels address more advanced technical and psychological issues that help to realize successful performances.

 Use the enclosed CD as a teaching and motivational tool. Have your students listen to the recording and discuss interpretation with you!

Production: Frank and Gail Hackinson
Production Coordinators: Philip Groeber and Isabel Otero Bowen
Cover: Terpstra Design, San Francisco
Cover Piano Illustration: Keith Criss
Text Design and Layout: Maritza Cosano Gomez
Engraving: Kevin Olson and Tempo Music Press, Inc.
Printer: Tempo Music Press, Inc.

ISBN 1-56939-447-4

9 Recital Preparation Tips • For the Teacher

1. Consider a tiered approach to developing comfort in performance. Make "mini" performances a regular occurrence, probably without even calling them performances. Have a student play for the student who follows his/her lesson. It doesn't matter if their leveling is different; the older students are naturally nice to the young and the young provide a non-threatening audience for the older. Have students play mini concerts at home. Younger students may enjoy concerts for their favorite stuffed animals each day after practice. Advise older students to practice performing by recording themselves. Of course, you will tailor these suggestions according to each student's personality. Just remember, *no venue is too small and frequency is the key*. Suggestions for mini-performances and performance strategies are also addressed on pages 13, 18, 19, and 27.

   Once students are comfortable with these "mini" performances, teachers must create opportunities for students to play in public, so that they will get used to the idea of getting up on stage and playing for others. Studio group lessons or performance classes are perfect for trial performances, then take it to the next step and invite family or friends to a performance class.

   Try these different performance venues and you will be pleased with the results. The "tiered" approach helps performance to become a natural part of piano study.

2. Make sure that your students have the opportunity to perform pieces well within their technical range. These performances will help build student confidence and will make a huge difference when they are playing more challenging repertoire.

3. Have students practice concentrating on the tempo, mood, and dynamics of the piece before beginning to play.

4. Coach students on how to walk purposefully *to* the piano, adjust the bench, and check their position relative to the piano. Have them practice this a lot in the lesson and at home. Familiarity with the process really helps.

5. Talk to your students about how to finish the piece. Coach them to stay with the music until the piece is over. Discuss how they will move at the end of the piece: i.e., quickly moving the hands away from the keyboard, or slowly lifting the hands with the lifting of the pedal, depending on the repertoire.

6. Coach students how to bow and walk purposefully *away* from the piano. Again, practice this together often so that it feels natural to them.

7. Remind students to keep the recital in perspective. The recital piece should be one of several the student is working on, so that they understand that there is "life after the recital."

8. If possible, have a practice session in the performance location. Encourage your students to focus on what they can control and remind them that although a piano may feel differently, their technique will not "go away."

9. Have your students listen to the companion CD. Not only does this give them ideas on how to interpret the pieces, it builds an intuitive knowledge of how the pieces sound, which helps increase confidence and comfort.

The goal is to instill in our students the excitement of playing for others and to demystify the process. There is nothing quite like communicating a piece of music to an audience and then enjoying their positive reaction to it. With our help, our students can perform up to their potential in public and enjoy this exciting and rewarding experience.

ORGANIZATION OF THE SERIES
IN RECITAL™ • THROUGHOUT THE YEAR

*I*n Recital™ — *Throughout the Year* is carefully leveled into the following categories: Early Elementary, Elementary, Late Elementary, Early Intermediate, Intermediate, and Late Intermediate. Each of the works has been selected for its artistic as well as its pedagogical merit.

Book Six — Late Intermediate, reinforces the following concepts:

- Rhythmic patterns of dotted eighth notes, sixteenth notes, and triplet sixteenth notes.

- Pieces in simple, compound, and mixed meters.

- More challenging passage work, scales in tenths, octaves, glissandos, and hand-over-hand configurations.

- One piece introduces impressionistic style with parallel chords, color chords, and the use of the middle pedal.

- Pieces with changes of tempo, character, and articulations.

- Students play pieces in which the melody and the accompaniment are found within the same hand.

- Syncopated rhythms, jazz chords, and all kinds of arpeggiated and broken chord patterns appear.

- Simple ornamentation is used such as grace notes and trills.

- Pieces reinforce the following musical terms: *espressivo, cantando, melancolico, teneramente, accelerando, rallentando, più mosso, meno mosso,* along with basic musical terminology found in books 1-5.

- A mixture of major and minor keys strengthen the student's command of the piano.

All but one of the pieces in Book Six are solos. *Toreador Song* is arranged as an equal part duet.

TABLE OF CONTENTS

FF1464

FIRST SNOWFALL

Melody Bober

Toccata and Fugue in D Minor

BWV 565

J. S. Bach
arr. Kevin Olson

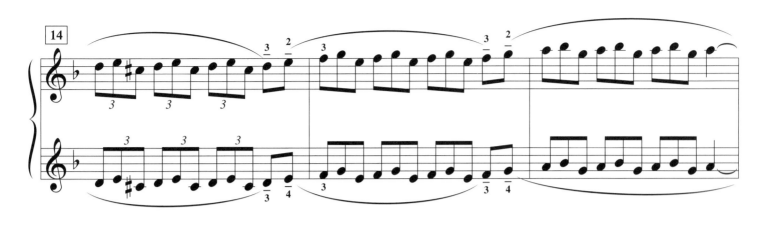

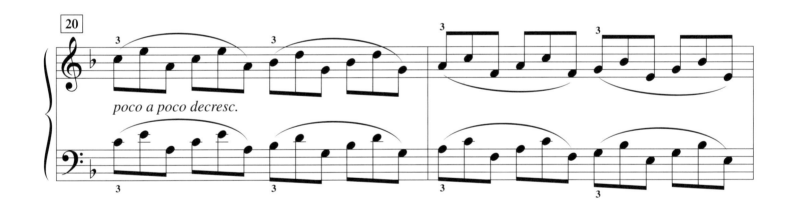

Good Preparation = Successful Performance

Try these five performance tips:

1. Play your piece through without stopping. Pretend you are playing in the recital. If you make a little mistake, just keep going. This practice strategy helps you to learn how you will feel when you are performing your piece(s) in a recital.

   Then, think about the following questions and answer them below:

   Did I play my piece(s) steadily, making sure that it was rhythmically accurate? (Could I easily hear every single note in the piece?) If not, what could I have done better?

   _____

   Did I play my piece(s) beautifully, with a good sound at every moment? If not, what could I have done better?

   _____

As the performance date gets closer, try to play your piece *three times without stopping* every day. Then, try the following:

2. Practice only sections of your piece. One rule of thumb to remember is to play a section three times slowly, paying careful attention to all of the details (rhythm, tempos, dynamics, etc.), and then one time, "a tempo."

3. Record yourself. This will give you the feeling of performing in front of others, even though you are playing only for yourself.

4. Listen to the CD recording of your recital piece. How does this help you to play your piece even better?

5. Play in front of an audience. This is part of the fun of learning how to play the piano — to share the music with others!

Write below the four places along with the dates of where you performed your piece(s) *before* the recital.

   _____

   _____

   _____

   _____

> You can use this page as a practice guide for every recital piece you play in this book!

to Melinda Clara Groves

ROMANZA

Martín Cuéllar

Andante espressivo (♩ = 92)

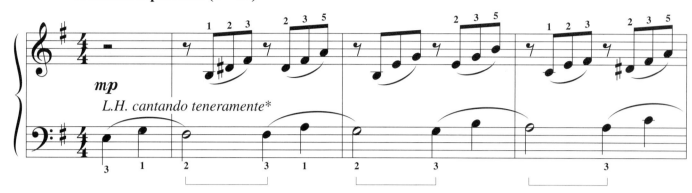

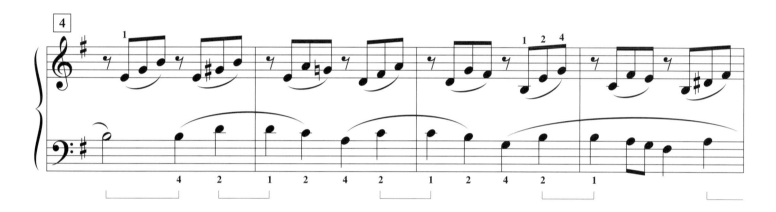

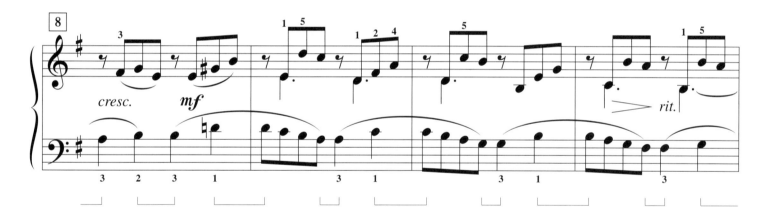

* singing with tenderness

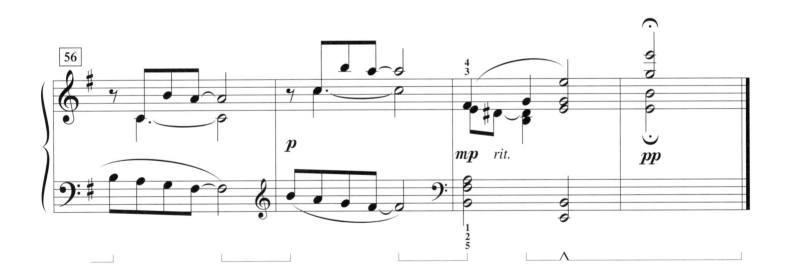

MANAGING PERFORMANCE JITTERS

Here are a few things to think about before you perform. It is important to think about them well in advance of the performance, so that you feel great about the performance when it comes!

> *The greatest freedom in playing comes from the most disciplined preparation...*

- **Stay** in the moment.

- **Don't** judge yourself.

- **Don't** think of what happened or what might happen.

- **Think** about the importance of a steady beat and an appropriate tempo.

- **Concentrate** on what you can control, and don't worry about what you can't.

- **Assess** your performance after you play, not *during*.

- **Think** positive scenarios about your playing; then imagine yourself playing your recital piece beautifully.

- **Keep** the performance in perspective and enjoy it! Every performance is a learning experience!

> You can use these pages as a practice guide for every recital piece you play in this book!

Preparing for a recital is like throwing
darts at the bull's eye.

Follow these practice steps:

- Mark off small sections of your recital piece. Play one of the sections. Every time you play something incorrectly, mark a place on one of the circles of the dartboard around the bull's eye. If you play something absolutely correctly, mark the bull's eye. When you miss the bull's eye we call it "learning" the piece. When you can hit the bull's eye consistently, then you are "practicing."

- Try to earn a "bull's eye" five times in a row, practicing the exact same small section of your recital piece.

- The more you practice, the better your mark will be at earning a bull's eye. Soon you will be able to get a bull's eye 6 times in a row, or 7, or 8 times! Use this strategy, it works!

To learn **What Makes a Performance Stellar**, turn to page 27.

Toreador Song

from the opera, *Carmen*

Secondo

Georges Bizet
arr. Edwin McLean

Allegro molto moderato (♩ = ca. 112)

Toreador Song

from the opera, *Carmen*

Primo

Georges Bizet
arr. Edwin McLean

Allegro molto moderato ($\quad$ = ca. 112)

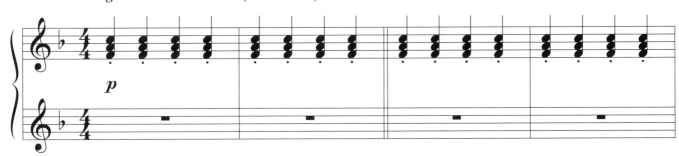

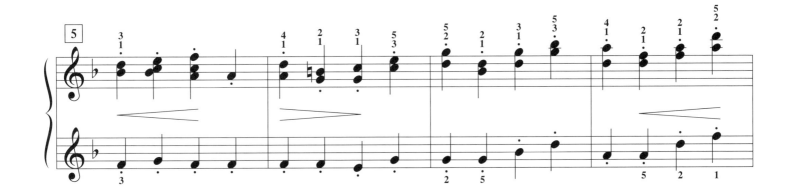

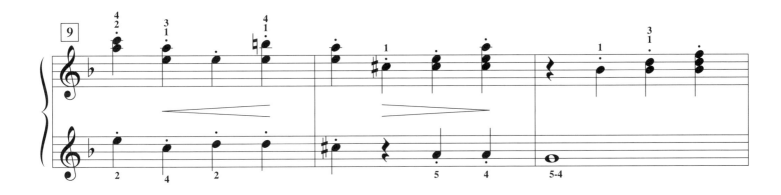

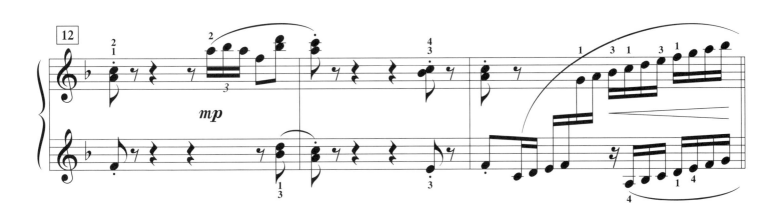

FF1464

Secondo

Primo

Bagatelle

Timothy Brown

26

FF1464

What Makes a Performance Stellar?

Starting four weeks before your actual performance, practice the following performance strategies every day. It might be difficult to do all of these at first, but the more you practice, the easier they will become. Remember, if you prepare well, the performance day will be easy and your playing will amaze your audience!

Place a check in the box each day you complete the task.

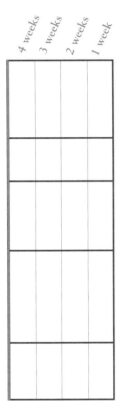

Can you play the entire piece, hands alone? (Listening to each individual part helps you to be completely aware of what each hand is playing.)

Can you sing or hum the melody away from the piano?

Can you start your piece at four *different* places in the music? (You and your teacher can mark with a star ☆ four good starting places).

Can you play the piece from beginning to end at "half tempo"? ("Half tempo" means to play it with all of the correct rhythms, notes, and dynamics, but at half of the speed you would play it when performing it.)

After playing the piece, ask yourself: Did it sound like the title suggests? Did I bring the piece to life?

Other questions you can ask yourself:

- Do I play all of the dynamics as the composer intended them to be?
- Do I play with all of the correct articulations? (not too sticky or too quick)
- Do I give the notes their exact duration?
- Are the *ritardandos* and *accelerandos* in the right places?
- Is my sound beautiful?
- Is my passage work clear?
- Have I worked to control all of the soft or slow passages?
- Can I play my recital piece without the pedal — dry and with complete accuracy?

> You can use this page as a practice guide for every recital piece you play in this book!

Jingle Bell Jam

Kevin Olson

Dans le jardin

(In the Garden)

Timothy Brown

* Editor's note: if playing on a grand piano, you can experiment with depressing the *sostenuto* pedal
for more impressionistic color.

FF1464

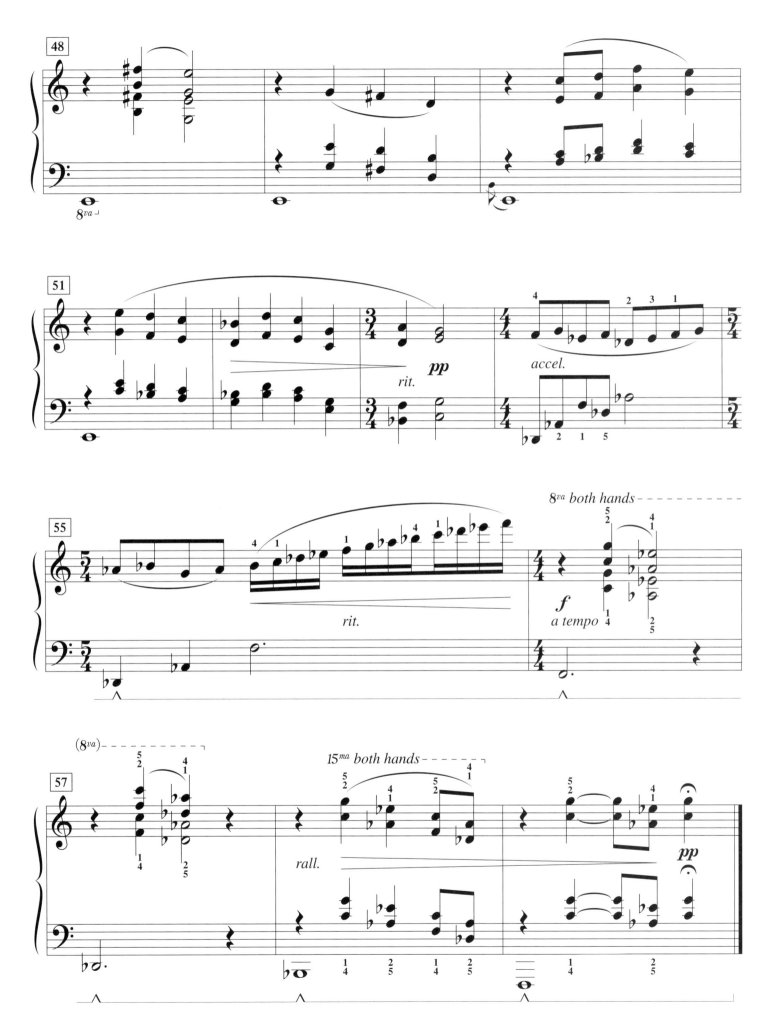

Toccatina

David Karp

ABOUT THE COMPOSERS/ARRANGERS

Melody Bober

Piano instructor, music teacher, composer, clinician—Melody Bober has been active in music education for over 25 years. As a composer, her goal is to create exciting and challenging pieces that are strong teaching tools to promote a lifelong love, understanding, and appreciation for music. Pedagogy, ear training, and musical expression are fundamentals of Melody's teaching, as well as fostering composition skills in her students.

Melody graduated with highest honors from the University of Illinois with a degree in music education, and later received a master's degree in piano performance. She maintains a large private studio, performs in numerous regional events, and conducts workshops across the country. She and her husband Jeff reside in Minnesota.

Timothy Brown

Composition has always been a natural form of self-expression for Timothy Brown. His Montessori-influenced philosophy has greatly helped define his approach as a teacher and composer of educational music. His composition originates from a love of improvisation at the piano and his personal goal of writing music that will help release the student's imagination.

Mr. Brown holds two degrees in piano performance, including a master's degree from the University of North Texas. His many honors include a "Commissioned for Clavier" magazine article, and first prize award in the Fifth Aliénor International Harpsichord Competition for his solo composition *Suite Española*. As a clinician, Mr. Brown has presented numerous clinics and most recently represented FJH Music with his presentation at the 2000 World Piano Pedagogy Conference. Currently living in Dallas, Mr. Brown teaches piano and composition at the Harry Stone Montessori Magnet School. He frequently serves as an adjudicator for piano and composition contests, and performs with his wife as duo-pianists.

Martín Cuéllar

Pianist Martín Cuéllar is Assistant Professor of Piano at Emporia State University in Emporia, Kansas. He received his Doctor of Musical Arts and Master of Music degrees in piano performance from The University of Texas at Austin. As a rotary scholar, Dr. Cuéllar studied at The Royal Conservatory of Music in Madrid, Spain, where he received the diploma in piano performance. He has done additional research and piano studies on the music of Enrique Granados at the Marshall Academy of Music in Barcelona, Spain. His edition of Enrique Granados' Valses Poéticos, published by The FJH Music Company, enjoys universal, critical acclaim.

An active performer, Dr. Cuéllar plays concerts throughout the United States, Mexico, Brazil, and Spain. He is a member of the National Guild of Piano Teachers, chair of the guild's International Piano Composition Contest, and adjudicator for the organization both nationally and internationally. Many of his piano compositions are on the required repertoire list of the National Federation of Music Clubs. Martín Cuéllar currently resides in Emporia, Kansas, with his wife and two children.

David Karp

Dr. David Karp—nationally known pianist, composer, and educator—holds degrees from Manhattan School of Music and the University of Colorado. He has also done graduate work at Teachers College, Columbia University. Dr. Karp is currently professor of music at SMU's Meadows School of the Arts and director of the National Piano Teachers Institute.

As a clinician and adjudicator, Dr. Karp has traveled the United States from Alaska to New Hampshire, as well as internationally. He has been a guest conductor and commissioned composer for the New Hampshire Summer Piano Camp at Plymouth State University, and was recently honored with the establishment of the David Karp Piano Festival, which is held each spring at Kilgore College. In June 2002, Dr. Karp served on the panel of judges for the Van Cliburn International Piano Competition for Outstanding Amateurs.

Edwin McLean

Edwin McLean is a composer living in Coconut Grove, Florida. He is a graduate of the Yale School of Music, where he studied with Krzysztof Penderecki and Jacob Druckman. He also holds degrees in music theory and piano performance from the University of Colorado.

Mr. McLean is the recipient of several grants and awards, including The MacDowell Colony, the John Work Award, the Woods Chandler Prize (Yale), Meet the Composer, Florida Arts Council, and others. He has also won the Aliénor Composition Competition for his work Sonata for Harpsichord, published by The FJH Music Company Inc. and recorded by Elaine Funaro (Into the Millennium, Gasparo GSCD-331).

Since 1979, Edwin McLean has had a busy career in music publishing. He has arranged the music of some of today's best known recording artists. Currently, he is senior editor as well as MIDI orchestrator for FJH Music.

Kevin Olson

Kevin Olson is an active pianist, composer, and faculty member at Elmhurst College near Chicago, Illinois, where he teaches classical and jazz piano, music theory, and electronic music. He holds a Doctor of Education degree from National-Louis University, and bachelor's and master's degrees in music composition and theory from Brigham Young University. Before teaching at Elmhurst College, he held a visiting professor position at Humboldt State University in California.

A native of Utah, Kevin began composing at the age of five. When he was twelve, his composition An American Trainride received the Overall First Prize at the 1983 National PTA Convention in Albuquerque, New Mexico. Since then, he has been a composer-in-residence at the National Conference on Piano Pedagogy and has written music for the American Piano Quartet, Chicago a cappella, the Rich Matteson Jazz Festival, among others. Kevin maintains a large piano studio, teaching students of a variety of ages and abilities. Many of the needs of his own piano students have inspired his nearly forty books and solos published by The FJH Music Company Inc., which he joined as a writer in 1994.